The infinite mindset

BÜCHER BERISHA

Flamur Berisha

About the author

Flamur Berisha, was born on 15.01.1992. Non-fiction author for psychology. After completing numerous seminars, he decided to specialize in the field of personalities and their development in 2014. He finds the subject fascinating, as people are capable of things, that they don't know of yet. He informs and supports his readers in order for them to achieve goals that they are for from as of now. Every person is capable of learning and has the capability to grow out of themselves and further develop. So that everyone can experience these developments, he informs with his books on personality development and gives many valuable tips.

Foreword

What if everything you wanted for your life were within your grasp? Do you think it is possible that only the nature of your mindset determines whether your dreams and visions can be lived and realized?

If you have believed until now that your happiness in life depends on external factors, with this book you hold the key to your new consciousness in your hands: Because you create your reality! You alone are the creator of your happiness in life! With the right attitude, you too can become a magnet for success, happiness, love and contentment! And for this you actually do not need much. Every person can create a powerful mindset with a little practice. And this is the basis for a life complete of fulfillment. This guidebook, will supply you with step-by-step instructions for creating your personal success mindset. You will learn what is important in mindset work and which role goals, self-awareness, positive thinking, happiness, self-discipline and motivation play.

With the help of a variety of practical tips and exercises, your mindset will be transformed bit by bit as you work through this book. You will not only learn to see the world with different eyes.

Step by step, you will create the life you want from the bottom of your heart.

Are you ready for it? Then let's get started!

Mindset

WHAT IS MINDSET

When you set out to steer your life in a happy and successful direction, there is no way around your "own mindset". You have probably come across this term before. Maybe you have already dealt with your personal mindset. But what is a "mindset"? It sounds like quite a big deal at first, don't you think? Let's take a closer look at what's behind it.

The term "mindset" is a combination of the two words "mind" and "set". So in general, you could say that your "mindset" is something like the "composition of your mind" or your "set of thoughts". In case you don't really have an idea of what this - in my opinion very apt - image means, let's be more specific: Understand the term "mindset" as a paraphrase for "the way you conceive yourself and the world". Other terms could be:

- Mindset
- Mentality
- Attitude
- Worldview

A Mindset - or just a world view, attitude, mentality - arises from the sum of all experiences that a person has made in his life. It is composed of the very own imprints and values that each individual has acquired over the course of his life in exchange with his environment. Depending on whether a person has had predominantly positive or negative experiences with their environment, they develop their own individual mindset.

You surely know from yourself or from your environment, that the way people think about themselves and encounter their environment can differ in many ways. This ultimately becomes visible in the way someone shapes his or her life. For example, while one person is more critical and cautious, another is more ambitious or particularly helpful towards other people. I am sure that you can easily continue these examples and apply them to yourself and other people around you. In everyday life, we are all permanently confronted with many different peoples ways of thinking, attitudes or world views. You may have noticed in your everyday life that you sometimes feel irritated or even annoyed by others attitudes, positions and ways of thinking. This is the ground on which disputes and conflicts are carried out. So, when you have a dispute with someone, you could say that your two mindsets simply don't match.

However, there is also a completely different phenomenon that I'm sure you're familiar with: Sometimes we are in contact with other people who impress or inspire us with their mindsets and attitudes. For example, you may have a work colleague whom you admire for remaining calm even in the most stressful situations. Or you have a friendship with someone who inspires you with his or her ambition, success, or contented partnership. And you wonder how he or she does it and why you might find it harder to deal with certain situations.

You probably already guessed it: the key to this lies in your mindset. At this point, there is good news for you! Your mindset is not set in stone. You can change it and steer it in the direction you want. Your mindset can be changed. You can constantly develop it further and thus create the life you want for yourself in the long term. Can you still not believe that it could be so simple? Then you will learn in the further course why your Mindset is unlimited and what you have to do to tap into your very own, dynamic and infinite Mindset.

WHY THE MINDSET IS INFINITE

As you have experienced up to this point, every human being has a very individual way of understanding himself and his world. Every person has his own mindset, which in principle reflects all experiences made with his environment. Looking back on your life, you may find that your wide range of experiences also includes negative experiences. This is normal. Every one of us has experienced hardships and disappointments over the course of our lifes.

These can now affect your present life by influencing your mindset, your way of thinking. For example, the experience of repeatedly failing to perform well at school in childhood can have an effect on developing a suitable mindset. This could then become visible in the fact that someone is also worried in adulthood about not being good enough or not setting professional goals for fear of not being able to achieve them. Another person who has experienced little love during his or her upbringing, may develop a mindset that prevents them from building loving relationships and contacts. But since these are essential for every human being, it is possible that they could start suffering, in the long run.

Now, of course, we cannot change the past and have to live with the experiences we have had up to this point. What we can change, however, is the way we evaluate and process experiences. Because to be able to fully grasp the emergence of a mindset, we have to go one step further at this point.

Different people can deal with the same situation in absolutely different ways. If we think of the aforementioned colleague who remains calm in stressful situations, while we ourselves may quickly loose our balance, this becomes clear. Now, let's assume that this fictitious colleague has had experiences in his life that have shaped his mindset in such a way that pressure from outside does not lead to him becoming unbalanced. Perhaps, he has a fundamental knowledge that all plans and goals he made, can be realized. Or he has a deep confidence in his own competence. In any case, it can be assumed that he does not view the situation as particularly threatening, which ultimately enables him to deal with it in a more relaxed manner.

So, it is the way how we evaluate situations and experiences that ultimately affects how we experience and process experiences.

Feel free to read this sentence again. Because it is THE twist to successfully working with your unlimited mindset. Again:

Your Mindset is the foundation for how you understand yourself and the world and how you shape your life accordingly. Your existing mindset is composed of all the experiences you have had in your life so far. At the same time, the perception and interpretation of all present and future situations takes place through your personal "mindset glasses". You can imagine this as a kind of filter that only lets through stimuli that fit into the existing scheme. Unsuitable information simply rushes past and is not taken up by you at all.

What does this mean for you and your mindset? It means that with a little practice you can specifically adjust and focus your mindset glasses.

And you can do it in such a way that your perception is directed to the stimuli and information that have otherwise just passed you by. It is not the case that we are helplessly at the mercy of our past mindset programming and must accept it as the result of our past.

We always have a choice in how we evaluate ourselves and our experiences. We can direct our focus to perceive situations positively and optimistically. This requires some practice. In addition, it is first necessary to subject your existing mindset programming to a critical review. Only when you have recognized your programming, your very own patterns, and can see where they are slowing you down, can you shift your focus.

Only then can you specifically adjust your mindset glasses the way you want. To illustrate this, let's go back to the example of "dealing with stress": Let's assume that you have recognized for yourself that you are easily upset by stressful situations. Then first analyze your existing mindset: What triggers stress in you? Which patterns are activated?

Perhaps you will find that you have deeply internalized the idea that you must not disappoint the expectations of others. Or you become aware of the fact that you have the feeling that you cannot cope with tasks because of certain experiences.

This, by the way, is often what triggers stress in us. We perceive an insurmountable discrepancy between the tasks to be accomplished and our own competencies. This causes the feeling of stress.

Now, once you have identified the particular programming of your mindset that is related to your feelings of stress, you can bypass or override it. For example, you might find for yourself that you have doubts about your competence because of past experiences. Then you could work on your self-confidence and direct your focus specifically to your strengths and successes. You might also become aware of the fact that it is difficult for you to distance yourself from external expectations and to stay with yourself. Maybe it could help you to learn a relaxation technique and to practice how to always come back to yourself with your focus

What should be made clear with this exemplary presentation is: *Humans are beings capable of learning.* We have the ability and also the fundamental possibility to constantly learn new things. This is the reason why we can constantly reprogram and develop our mindset. The example is transferable to all conceivable life situations and behavior patterns.

How do you feel now with this knowledge? Did you feel, while reading, that your brain is being directed into new ways of thinking?

Speaking of the brain. What role does it actually play for our mindset?

What happens in our brain?

According to a recent study by researchers at Queens University in Kingston, each person thinks an average of 6,200 thoughts a day. That's quite a lot. You'll be familiar with it: From going through the grocery list to mentally preparing for the important conversation with the boss - in principle, we are busy thinking about something throughout our entire daily lives.

But why do we think so much? Let's take a look at how the dictionary of psychology and education defines "thinking": *"Thinking as a mental activity can be associated with information processing, knowledge acquisition and problem solving, whereby problem solving is of great importance. Every human being is able to think, although the abilities may vary from person to person."*

So, as we can see, our brain uses thinking processes to help us process information, develop new ideas, and solve problems.

To do this, you have to consider that we are all exposed to millions of stimuli every day, which we have to allocate in our system. In connection with this, we are all permanently confronted with situations that require a reaction or our action. Let me put it another way:

You are standing at a traffic light, you see that it is red, and stop. At the same time, you may realize that you are running late today and may miss your bus.

So, as soon as the light turns green, you will make sure to pick up your pace and thus be able to catch the bus.

This common everyday situation may make it clear to you what your brain is actually doing all day. It processes stimuli from the outside, sorts them according to your inner system, becomes aware of possible problems and takes care of finding a solution for them. Pretty impressive, isn't it?

Types of thinking

We have already seen that there are many different ways of thinking about yourself and your environment. In other words, there are many different ways to think about yourself and the world. Depending on personal experiences and one's own self-concept, but also on external factors, each person has his or her own individual perspective on the world. Every person looks through his or her own personal mindset glasses.

As diverse as people are, so are their ways of thinking. It is therefore difficult to categorize mindsets unambiguously. However, the goal of this guide is to direct your focus on developing a powerful mindset. To do this, it is necessary for you to become aware of fundamental differences that can exist in thinking.

You can then use this knowledge to check your personal mindset glasses for alignment. Eventually, you will be able to align your thoughts and focus so that you can draw into your life all that you desire.

To do this, first realize that all the diverse and completely different ways of thinking of different people can be roughly divided into:

Positive ways of thinking

or

Negative ways of thinking.

This means that people tend to perceive themselves and the world around them either in a *positive, hopeful* way or in a *negative, critical way*.

Take a look at your circle of friends, acquaintances and colleagues. What kind of people are you surrounded with? Do you predominantly know people who see the glass as half empty and tend to discontent, mistrust or despondency? Or are you surrounded by people who consciously shape their lives and are characterized by a benevolent and optimistic attitude towards life? What about yourself? Are you more of a positive thinker who can see and seize opportunities? Or do you tend to let worries and discouragement keep you from achieving your goals?

If so, don't fret. Because with this guidebook, you already hold the key to your success in your hands. You can change the way you think! You can change your mindset! To do this, it is necessary to analyze your previous thinking patterns and reprogram them step by step. In the course of this guidebook you will receive numerous incentives that will eventually lead you to a powerful and infinite mindset. First, realize that there are certain factors that influence the way we think. If you know what they are, you can consciously use this knowledge to positively influence the way you think. Let's take a look at the main factors below.

Factors influencing the way we think

Stress

One essential element that should not be underestimated in its effect on our thought patterns is stress. Our performance-oriented society demands a lot from us. The demands on our professional and private lives are increasing, our cell phones are constantly ringing, and our schedules are full.

All of this not only means that we automatically increase the demands we place on ourselves. It also means that we run the risk of losing ourselves in all our appointments and external expectations.

This is because our brain is basically subject to constant input. In addition to permanently processing stimuli, it must continuously solve complex problems. The carousel of thoughts runs at full speed. It then becomes increasingly difficult to take a break from thinking and relax after work. What's more, when we have a lot to do and little opportunity to relax, it becomes increasingly difficult to maintain a positive outlook. You will certainly be familiar with this.

To maintain an optimistic outlook, it is therefore more important than ever to develop good strategies for dealing with stress. This includes, for example, taking regular time out to recharge your batteries. Learning a relaxation method (e.g. yoga, meditation or progressive muscle relaxation) can also be useful.

Emotions

The way we think is significantly influenced by our emotions.

I'm sure you're familiar with this: When you're not feeling well, sad, tired or angry, it's harder to keep a positive outlook on things.

For example, let's say you've just been dumped by your partner. Logically, you feel sad and perhaps inferior for having been abandoned. In this phase, you will understandably find it more difficult to focus on positive aspects and strengths. Instead, you will think of all the experiences in which you have been rejected. Our brain is structured in this way. If we find ourselves in an depressed emotional state, our brain automatically reactivates memories of situations in which we have been in similar states. Access to positive experiences and self-perceptions is more difficult in this state.

The good news is that this also works the other way around: So, for example, if you are newly in love and think you are the king of the jungle, it is automatically easier for you to perceive yourself and the world as positive. You then have "rose-colored glasses" on - ever heard of that?! In this state everything is wonderful, everything is feasible, worries and suffering are miles away and have nothing at all to do with your life.

Now, of course, you cannot and should not influence your life in such a way that you only float on clouds. That would be nice at first sight, but it would not correspond to our life. Because lows are just as much a part of it as highs. Negative feelings are also part of it, and it should not be the goal to no longer want to have them and to suppress them. Because that makes you sick.

However, you can decide for how long and how deep you want to dive into negative feelings. Because you now have the awareness that in a negative emotional state it will be more difficult for you to think positively about yourself and to look to the future with hope. At the same time, you know that you will find it easier to create new goals as soon as you feel better.

So you can use this knowledge to consciously work your way back out of negative feelings. Because then the clouds in your head will also automatically move to the side. There are a few ways to encourage yourself to feel more positive. A very effective one is to specifically trigger feelings of happiness in yourself.

Feelings of happiness

The perception of feelings of happiness automatically leads to a positive coloring of our thought structures. When we feel happy, we perceive ourselves and our surroundings more positively and look to our future with more hope and courage.

So what could be more obvious than to consciously evoke feelings of happiness? Exactly. Nothing.

The only question is, how can you trigger feelings of happiness in yourself? Well, just in case you might not be newly in love. To do this, it is first important to know where feelings of happiness actually come from and what they do in our bodies.

Certain hormones and messenger substances are responsible for the sensation of happiness. Our body releases these in specific situations. When we are in love, for example, oxytocin is released in high quantities. This not only makes us happy, but also promotes the desire to commit to the partner.

Other essential happiness messengers include serotonin and dopamine. We can specifically trigger their release, even if right now we are not in a (newly in love) relationship:

- As soon as you move or actively participate in sports, your body releases a multitude of happiness-inducing messenger substances, including serotonin and dopamine.

So if you want to specifically trigger feelings of happiness in yourself, do a round of **sports**: go for a jog, go for a bike ride, join an aerobics class, jump rope, dance around your apartment... These are all not only excellent ways to relieve stress. Your body will also reward you with an extra dose of happiness. And if you don't want to do a complete workout, **a walk in the fresh air** will also do. Even moderate exercise outside will improve your mood.

- Trigger feelings of happiness in yourself by making yourself **laugh**. You think that sounds crazy? Actually, it doesn't. Because as soon as you laugh, your body receives the signal to release serotonin and dopamine. Why not take advantage of this knowledge and give your own happiness a boost? So consciously watch a funny series that leaves you no choice but to laugh. Or if you can - treat yourself to being really silly. There are even laughing yoga courses. These aim to encourage participants to laugh and, in this way, lead them to their sincere joy. Maybe there's a class near you - then give it a try.

- The **way we eat** also has an effect on our mood. It is now known that a certain diet leads to an increase in serotonin levels. This includes fish, for example, but also foods rich in carbohydrates and low in protein. In other words, lots of cereal products, legumes and, in moderation, also meat. In the further course of this guide, you will receive further concrete tips for a balanced and energy-giving diet.

- Last but not least, any kind of **physical closeness** naturally leads to the release of oxytocin and thus to a feeling of happiness. If you have a partner, treat yourself to a conscious cuddle session. If you don't have a partner, hugs from friends or cuddling your pet can have the same effect.

So what is needed

for an infinite mindset?If you have read this far, you already have all the knowledge you need to develop your mindset to infinity. Basically, the expansion of the Mindset takes place through:

- **Analyzing your current mindset structure**: In order to be able to develop your mindset into infinity, you must first become aware of its current structure. How do you perceive yourself and your environment? Are you more someone who sees the glass as half full or half empty? How do the people you surround yourself with think? What experiences in your life have led you to have this one view of things?

All of these questions can give you approaches to get a picture of your personal way of thinking. Always keep in mind that your view is not set in stone. You can change it. Once you are clear about your perspective, you can consciously shift it to where you want to go.

- **The conscious change of your focus**: This is ultimately the key to the infinity of your mindset. Thus, the alignment of your focus alone decides whether you will be

- happy or unhappy,
- successful or despondent,
- a creator of your own reality or a victim of circumstances.

You alone have the power to direct your focus specifically where you want to go. Once you have internalized this, you can see that your mindset is infinite - depending on what goal you want to achieve, you can develop your mindset to go exactly there.

Again, once you know what you want to achieve and who you want to be, you can direct your focus specifically to achieving those goals!

Maybe you stumble across one or two ingrained thought patterns along the way that are holding you back from achieving your goals. Then work on it! You may also become aware that you are missing specific knowledge or skills that you still need to reach this goal. Then acquire them!

Maybe it is necessary to change your previous routines to get closer to what you want to achieve. For example, by specifically integrating sports and conscious nutrition into your life. In any case, you have the power over how you align your mindset. And with it, what kind of life you lead.

In the further course of this guide, you will receive step-by-step instructions on how to unlock your unlimited mindset. Essential elements on this path are:

- Goals
- Self-confidence
- Positive thinking
- Self-discipline
- Motivation

Each individual point is described and explained in more detail below. In addition, you will receive concrete tips and practical approaches for each topic, which you can use for your individual mindset work. The five aspects influence and complement each other. Their holistic interaction leads to the infinite expansion of your personal mindset. And with it putting your life on the road to success. Or to put it in the words of Albert Schweitzer:

"The greatest decision of your life lies in the fact that you can change your life by changing your mindset."

Goals

WHY SET GOALS

You now know that you are basically able to align your mindset. You also know about the possibility to do this in unlimited ways - depending on what you want to focus on. But how can you control this? How can you direct your focus in such a way that it leads to a powerful and successful mindset? Well, if you want to direct your focus - and thus also your mindset - in a specific direction, you first need one thing: concrete goals.

Where do you want to go? How do you want to be? What do you want to achieve? What do you want your life to be like in a year? These are all questions that can navigate you on the path to your new mindset. By becoming aware of what your current state is and what you want to change - compared to that - in the future, you automatically develop goals that you set. You may not necessarily be aware of it. But every vision of how you want your life to be in the future implies subliminal goal setting.

It is important to become aware of these often unconsciously occurring objectives. Only then can you make your goals visible and achievable. You can then plan concrete steps that you need to take to achieve your goals.

REAL GOALS AND ABSTRACT GOALS

Now, you can set very different goals. In principle, there are no limits to how you formulate your goals.

Maybe you want to reduce your weight in the next six months. Or you pursue the goal of earning more money. Or you want to become more self-confident. Maybe you want to take a longer vacation trip or finally get married.

The alignment of your goals - like the alignment of your mindset - is absolutely unlimited. Decisive for the development of your personal goals is your life situation, your personality structure and your individual value system.

No matter how big your dreams are and what concrete topic your objectives concern - there is one golden rule you should apply when formulating your goals:

Formulate your goals as concretely and realistically as possible!

For example, you might wish to be rich.

Financial security and prosperity are an issue for each of us, and the desire for wealth is thus a readily understandable goal. Good. So now you have your goal:

"I want to be rich."

Reads well at first, doesn't it? At the same time, however, this goal contains few concrete possibilities for action. However, these are needed for a goal to become attainable. The concretization of your goals decides that they do not remain as "unfulfilled castles in the sky".

The goal formulated above, *"I want to be rich"* is therefore an **abstract goal**. That means: You know that you want to be rich. But what does wealth actually mean to you? What possibilities are there for generating wealth? What could and would you have to do yourself to achieve this? These are all essential questions that you need to be aware of as part of your goal-setting process. Why? To better define your goal and thus to be able to establish its attainability in the first place.

When formulating your goals, it is therefore important that you check them for their concreteness and feasibility. On the one hand, this means that you formulate your goal as concretely as possible. Instead of *"I want to be rich"* it is better to formulate *"I want to increase my income by a total of 20% in the next 12 months."* Likewise, your goals should also be achievable.

For example, if you now set the goal *"I want to marry a millionair"* that may not be feasible. Now, of course, I don't know your private circumstances. And yes, with the right mindset you can certainly attract a wealthy partner in the long term. In any case, however, you should check with each goal whether there is a realistic prospect of its attainability. Or whether you might need to reword it to make it more tangible for you.

BIG GOALS AND SMALL GOALS

What you have just read should not discourage you. For God's sake, don't be afraid to have big goals and visions for your life. Because as I said before - basically, with the right mindset, you can achieve anything you want. And big goals are what is fueling this process. So go ahead and dream and develop unbridled visions of your future life. However, when it comes to the concrete feasibility, it makes sense to break your vision down into many small steps. Here's why: big, distant goals that are not really tangible for us, run the risk of remaining that way: big and distant. Or even worse: the feeling of not being able to reach these big goals - or not being able to reach them as quickly as we would have liked - can have a very demotivating and discouraging effect on us. You should be aware of this trap and avoid it.

Let me illustrate this with an example: Let's assume that you set yourself the goal of getting married in the next few years. You already see yourself in your inner eye on your big day. You already know at which special place the wedding should take place and perhaps you have already secretly planned your guest list. Only one essential ingredient is still missing: the right partner. Maybe you have been single for a short time, maybe for a long time.

The fact is: the desire and the idea of your own wedding are beautiful and legitimate. However, as long as there is no suitable partner in sight ,it remains a big undertaking.

I do not mean that you should stop imagining your dream wedding in the most dazzling colors at this moment. No, you should continue to do so! However, do not make the mistake of overlooking the intermediate steps. Because at worst, your big goal will make you feel bad about yourself if you still haven't sent out any invitation cards over the course of the next year.

Rather, it would make sense at this point to dedicate yourself to the intermediate steps. Before you can celebrate your dream wedding, you first need the right partner. That makes sense, doesn't it? Love is of course a very complex process and cannot be forced. But you could already help love finds its way a little bit.

For example, you could ask yourself what this partner should be like and where you could find him or her. You could go out more, join a sports club or a dating platform on the Internet. You could work on your self-confidence or appearance, if necessary, to increase your attractiveness to the opposite sex. You could start smiling at people you like on the street. And so on.

So you see, just up to the point of finding a relationship, the big goal of *"I want to get married."* could be broken down into many small sub-goals. If you become aware of these intermediate steps and formulate them for yourself as subgoals, you will be doing yourself a big favor.

Because:

- You make your project more concrete and tangible.
- You create opportunities to approach your big goal step by step.
- It is easier for you to take action.
- You can make visible progress by setting many small goals and mastering them step-by-step.
- This keeps you motivated while giving you the feeling that you can achieve your goals.

TYPES OF GOALS

Principally, there are different types of goals. You can set a wide variety of goals within each area of your life. The following are some examples:

Vocational

The purpose of setting professional goals is to shape the nature of one's occupation or to advance one's career. Possible goals are:

- I want to increase my sales by 20% within the next year.

- I want to work more from home.
- I would like to hold a management position in two years.
- …

Sports

Goals in sports refer to increasing your athletic performance. This can be, for example:

- I want to expand my jogging distance from 5 to 10 kilometers.
- I want to win 8 games during the season.
- I want to improve my time swimming by 20%.

Private (e.g. weight)

Private goals can relate to any other area of life that is meaningful to you. Conceivable goals are:

- I want to lose 3 kilos in the next 4 weeks.
- I want to expand my circle of friends and acquaintances.
- I want to work on my self-esteem.
- …

SET TIME PERIODS

In addition to specifying your goals, it also makes sense to set a time frame in which you want to achieve them. Being aware of how much time you will need to achieve your goal is an essential part of setting your goals in a proper way.

You consciously create a time window that you want to use for the development of your goal. At the same time, you create a motivation point to get into action. In the course of your time window you can check for yourself again and again how close you have already come to your goal and what you may still have to do to reach it by the end of your set deadline. Of course, it is also important here that you set the time frame as realistically as possible.

For example, if you want to lose weight as quickly as possible, it makes sense to think about how much weight you can realistically lose within a week or a month. For example, setting a goal of *"I want to lose twenty pounds in two weeks"* would be counterproductive, as you will probably not be able to do this in a healthy way. The consequence of this could be that you get a feeling of failure and discouragement. So, to keep your motivation up, rather formulate your goal in a way that makes it easy for you to achieve. For example, *"I want to lose six pounds in the next four weeks."* In this way, you give yourself a positive sense of achievement, which in turn affects your motivation and self-worth.

Basically, you can use the so-called **SMART formula** as a guide when formulating your goals. SMART stands for an American method for successful goal formulation. The term is an abbreviation.

SMART stands for: specific, measurable, attractive, realistic and time-bound. This means that when formulating goals, attention should be paid to these five aspects. Goals should be

- specific:

Concrete, subdivided into subgoals if necessary.

- measurable:

it should be measurable, e.g., "I want to lose five pounds." or "I want to generate 10% more income."

- attractive:

the attainability of the goal should have a positive connotation and not be perceived as "torturous"

- realistic:

Is closely related to attractiveness; it must be easily doable and attainable so that motivation to achieve it can be maintained

- time-bound:

A fixed period of time is set in order to maintain motivation and also to be able to control the achievement of the goal.

Why be self-confident at all?

WHAT DISTINGUISHES SELF-CONFIDENT PEOPLE

Self-confidence or self-awareness. What does that actually mean? Have you ever taken a closer look at the term *self-awareness*?

When we do, we realize that it is a compound word: Self-awareness. A *self-confident person* is therefore someone who is *aware* of his or herself. What could this mean?

According to the wording, it could mean someone who knows himself well. Furthermore, it could mean a person who is *conscious*. That is, someone who is aware of his strengths and weaknesses, imprints, needs and desires. Can you follow so far?

What about your self-awareness? Are you a person who is self-aware? How well do you know yourself? How do you present yourself to the world? How do you recognize a *self-aware person*?

Consider if you have someone in your circle of friends, acquaintances, or colleagues that you would describe as self-confident. How can you tell that this person is self-confident? How does he or she appear to you?

Basically, there are some visible characteristics that self-confident people possess. You can usually recognize self-confident people by the fact that they display at least the following three characteristics:

- They can assert themselves
- They make conscious decisions and act accordingly.
- They are able to say "no"

Assertiveness

If you have assertiveness, you are able to represent your own interests and needs to others and ultimately assert them. This does not mean to ignore the will of others and to focus only on oneself. That would be egoism. Rather, assertiveness describes the ability to present one's individual interests, goals or needs to another party. These are then presented in such a way that in the end the desired result is obtained. Assertiveness means standing up for oneself and having the courage to confront others. The basis for this is always fair communication at eye level and no use of power or pressure.

To be able to assert oneself, one must be aware of one's individual goals, interests, and needs. Furthermore, one must be convinced that their fulfillment will work and lead to an improvement of the situation.

Assertive people are characterized by a demeanor that conveys persuasiveness on the one hand, but also signals the ability to compromise on the other. The latter in particular leads to a kind of trust between the interlocutors. This is the basis for authentic assertiveness.

If you now realize that there is still room for improvement in your personal assertiveness, this is no reason to throw in the towel. Instead, start practicing! Use the next available opportunities for confrontation. Look for situations in which you must stand in for your interests and confornt the environment about it. Practice this. Experience yourself in these situations.

How do you feel when you stand up for yourself? Pay attention to how you speak, how you feel. How do you appear, what do you express non-verbally if necessary? Are you able to be assertive, fair, and willing to compromise at the same time?

Don't be afraid to constantly try out your assertiveness training. The questions raised can serve you as an orientation for self-observation. In particular, we will look at the importance of your body language in more detail later in this chapter.

Conscious decisions and actions

To be assertive - as we have already learned - you have to be aware of your inner goals, interests and needs. Only then can you represent them convincingly to the outside world. This leads us to another essential characteristic of self-confident people: the ability to make conscious decisions and to act according to them.

In order to make conscious decisions, you have to be clear about who you are and where you want to go. Here we go again: for purposeful decision-making, you have to be aware of yourself. This means regularly listening to yourself and comparing your goals, interests and needs with your current state. If it becomes clear that a change is needed to get closer to the personal motives again, the following applies: This change must be initiated. And a conscious decision must be made to do so. Let me illustrate this with an example:

If you are unhappy in your job, for example, this will become increasingly apparent to you. Maybe you don't feel like getting up in the morning anymore, or you are in a bad mood all the time. Maybe your performance is declining, or you feel that yourself is becoming more and more unenergetic. Noticing this requires a certain attention to yourself. If you further follow this process, you can feel inside yourself and ask yourself why you are increasingly in a bad mood or why your performance has dropped. You may then become aware of the fact that you find your work monotonous and that you lack a certain scope for further development.

However, you may also be suffering increasingly from conflict with your supervisor, which ultimately affects your overall motivation to work. Whatever it is, once you have become aware of it, you have reached an essential point: Now that you have located the root of your dissatisfaction, you can find a solution to this issue. You can make a conscious decision. This can then be, for example, the long overdue clarification talk with your superior or the search for a new fulfilling job.

Self-confident people not only remain constantly in touch with their inner motives and interests. As soon as they fade too much into the background, they check to what extent a balance can be restored. Finally, you come to a solution and make a decision. The next step is to act according to this decision. This requires a certain amount of courage and confidence in yourself. The decision you make must give you the feeling that it will improve the situation in the long term. And this in favor of one's own further development.

People who shape their lives in this way take full responsibility for themselves and their lives. They consciously take their lives into their own hands, make decisions and act proactively. They are not afraid of making mistakes or failing and live their lives in the form of a development process. You could say they are the designers of their own lives. If you would like to practice this a little more, your everyday life offers you a multitude of possibilities. Listen to yourself more often: What would you like to eat for breakfast? Do you really want to take the bus today or walk a bit? Do you really want to go to the movies tonight or do you feel more like relaxing on the sofa?

With the help of many small everyday situations you can sensitize your feeling for your needs and interests. Experience how it feels to act accordingly.

Saying no

Finally, this leads us to one last essential characteristic of self-confident people: the ability to say "no".

Many people struggle with turning down a request, canceling an appointment, or in any way being responsible that someone else's expectations are disappointed. This is because we mistakenly believe that the other party may equate our "no" with a rejection of their entire person.

The principle of meeting expectations usually stems from our childhood. From a time when we were more or less dependent on fulfilling the expectations of our parents and other caregivers. In principle, there is nothing wrong with being aware of other people's expectations and taking them into account in our own actions. However, most of us have derived a fatal fallacy from this: Namely, that other people's expectations have more weight than their own needs and interests.

41

This basic assumption is not found in the mindset of self-confident people! A self-confident person knows that he has the right to say "no". He further knows that this "no" says nothing about the other person. Rather, it expresses that someone here is aware of his own limits and values them. Taking oneself seriously. Against this background, the ability to say "no" is also an expression of one's own *self-awareness*. It testifies to knowing oneself and also remaining true to oneself - regardless of the expectations of others.

Before you can now object that such behavior could also be called egoism, let us be clear again: Similar to assertiveness, this is not about ignoring or overriding other people's perspectives. Rather, it is an incentive to sense one's own limits in an exchange with the other person and to stand up for them. Not ignorantly, but self-confidently. And above all, without the worry that you cannot "impose" your own limits on the other person. Because you can. Your primary responsibility should be to yourself, not to another person's boundaries.

Again, you will certainly have ample opportunity in your daily life to practice saying "no."

Pay attention to how you feel about it. Are you more with yourself or with the other person? What does it do to you when you stand up for yourself? In between, keep reminding yourself that you have the sole responsibility to protect your boundaries. Any - more or less - self-aware person should be able to handle this.

SHOW THE WORLD WHO YOU ARE

A self-confident person - this is how we can summarize up to this point - is therefore not only *aware of his self*, he also represents this to the outside world as a matter of course. He stands up for himself in every situation.

At this point, I would also like to invite you to stand up for yourself in every situation. More:

If you have so far been one of those people who prefer to stay in the background and not take up too much space, this is the time to stop doing so! If you have so far shied away from standing up for yourself and all your strengths, weaknesses and limitations, now is the right time to start!

Step out of your own shadow and show yourself to the world in all your colors and facets! Throw all your doubts, worries and fears overboard!

Have the courage to show yourself with all your corners and edges! Detach yourself from the fear of disappointing others or displeasing you! This is YOUR life!

If you want to follow along the way to your personal happiness and success, you must learn to believe in yourself, to stand up for yourself and to show yourself to the world! And don't worry: You have nothing to lose! By facing the world authentically, standing up for your interests, pursuing your goals and being aware of your limits, you can only win!

If you shape your life in this way, you will:

- gain self-confidence
- feel up to the challenges of your life
- develop a deep trust in yourself and the world
- have fulfilling relationships

- achieve professional success
- achieve everything you want

HOW CAN I STRENGTHEN MY SELF-AWARENESS?

If you've read this far and feel that this is exactly the life you want to lead - bingo, you've already got your mindset well aligned! However, insecurities and doubts may be surfacing within you. Can it all be that simple? How and where should I start showing myself to the world? What will my friends, my family say about it? Can I do it at all?

I can tell you this: Yes, you can! It may take some practice. But I am sure: If you really want it, you will become a person who confidently faces the world in any situation. What do you need for this? Exactly. A determined mindset. Following, you will get some approaches and methods that will help you to align your mindset properly and strengthen your self-confidence.

Self-observation (positive highlighting)

Do the following exercise regularly and be surprised by the effect it has on you. Consciously take a few minutes to look at yourself in peace. To do this, stand in front of a large mirror and look at yourself calmly. Look into your eyes, examine your face, smile at yourself.

Direct your focus to your teeth and hair, your ears and your neck. Let your gaze wander from mole to mole. Look carefully at your body, your shoulders and arms, your stomach, legs and feet. Pay attention to your toes and fingers as well. Of course, the same goes for your backside. Look at your back, your legs, your buttocks.

The important thing is to keep your focus on the positive. The point of this exercise is not to look at yourself critically. We all do that far too often. No. It's more about making yourself aware of your small and big beauties! What do you particularly like about yourself? Your eyes? Your hair? That one dimple when you smile? Maybe it's your belly button, a certain birthmark, or a meaningful tattoo? Every person has many beauties. Take the time to find yours! Become aware of your uniqueness and learn to increasingly look at yourself from loving eyes.

Self-analysis (What am I particularly good at?)

Conducting a self-analysis can further support you in focusing on your personal strengths and outstanding qualities. This exercise provides you with an additional tool for developing your positive and powerful mindset. To do this, it is a good idea to make a list. Give this list the heading "My strengths" or "What am I particularly good at?" and then get started. Write down everything that comes to mind. Everyone has strengths and special talents that set them apart from others. You too, I am sure. Take your time and think about what is easy for you or what you are particularly appreciated for.

For example:

- I am good at painting.
- I am good at handicrafts.
- I am good at parking.
- I am empathic.
- I notice quickly when someone has a new hairstyle/new clothes.
- I like to make others laugh.

- I am good at playing the guitar.
- I cook the best paella.

For your self-awareness and positive mindset, it is important that you are aware of your strengths. So feel free to read through your list often and also add to it regularly.

Daily affirmations

Where you direct your attention, that's where your life will be directed. You already know this. You can use this knowledge to "manipulate" yourself a little. Or better said: to direct your focus specifically. And that in a direction that feels good for you - towards happiness, success, love, contentment.

A wonderful method for this are *affirmations*. Affirmations are positive phrases and statements that you can say to yourself.

Examples are:

- I am lovable.
- I will stand up for my needs.
- I will be successful.
- I alone create my reality.
- Life is full of opportunities and possibilities.
- I am patient with myself.

See if you can identify with any of the above affirmations. Otherwise, let your imagination run wild. Look inside yourself.

- What do you wish for?
- What do you need?
- What do you want to focus on?

You can also look for inspiration on the Internet. There are a variety of affirmations in written or audio form (on YouTube, for example) that you can draw inspiration from. Find the affirmation(s) that are right for you and your current life situation. And then internalize it for yourself. There are several ways you can do this: Write down your affirmation(s) and post them in a visible place in your home or office. You can also develop a ritual out of it and recite or visualize your affirmation to yourself, e.g. every morning after getting up.

In this way, you consciously direct your focus on something positive. If you now repeat this regularly, you can increasingly anchor this positive perspective within yourself.

People learn through repetition. This means that in the long run, an affirmation routine will lead to your entire focus shifting increasingly towards the positive. This will automatically make it easier for you to perceive yourself and your life more positively.

Sport

It's already been mentioned: sports are a fantastic way to put yourself in a positive mood. In addition to the short-term high that sports activity triggers in our bodies, sports are also an essential element in boosting your self-confidence in the long run. For one thing, sport reduces stress to a high degree.

If you incorporate regular exercise into your daily routine, you will notice that you feel better overall and that you are more resilient. You will feel that it will be easier for you to "stay with yourself". In addition, sports have an immense impact on how we feel about our bodies. Depending on what sport you do - whether it's cycling, dancing, jogging, swimming or playing soccer - any type of sport challenges your body. More than that, sports serve to strengthen your body, to feel it.

If you exercise regularly, you will know that it has an effect on your posture. You will straighten your body more, feel the ground more firmly under your feet, and be more open in your overall posture.

You may even acquire a new pride in your body, due to the fact that you have been able to build up muscles here and there or lose a few kilos.

In short, regular exercise sessions will make you appear more determined and confident. This in turn will affect your self-esteem by automatically making you feel stronger and more present as well. So, in terms of your self-confidence, it is only advisable to adopt a regular sports routine. Take a look here to see what kind of sport appeals to you the most. Do you prefer to exercise alone or in a group with others? Do you prefer to be outdoors or indoors?

There's a wide range to explore between yoga and kickboxing, jump rope and soccer. Just try it out and experience what does you good. After all, it certainly takes some discipline to get into the habit of a sports routine. However, the basic idea of sporting activity should always remain the same - namely fun!

Reflect on your days (diary)

For a lasting increase in self-confidence, it can also be helpful to adopt a reflective routine, for example by keeping a diary. Consciously create a time window in the evening for this. Use this time for a more or less detailed daily reflection. Use the following questions as a guide:

- How are you feeling right now?
- How did your day go?
- Are you satisfied with yourself?
- What did you do well?

48

- What would you like to do differently next time?
- What positive impressions remain for you from this day?

If you reflect on your days in this way, you will train your self-confidence in the long term.

On the one hand, regularly reflecting on and writing down your daily routine helps you to understand yourself better: Your behavior patterns, your perspective on the world, your goals and needs. On the other hand, you can also practice directing your focus more and more positively.

Therefore, make sure not to be too strict with yourself in your daily reflection and to focus on positive experiences and small successes.

Rewards

You can link a positive daily reflection wonderfully by treating yourself to conscious rewards! Maybe you notice during your reflection routine that you have had a really challenging week. Maybe you can chalk up a successful development for yourself or see that you were able to overcome one of your hurdles. Whatever it is that your benevolent view of yourself brings to your attention - pay special attention to it! Reward yourself! Allow yourself something! Only for you and for the fact that you arrange your life exactly in such a way, as you do it!

By rewarding ourselves, we signal to ourselves that we are worth it. We send a signal to ourselves that we can see and appreciate our big and small accomplishments. This, in turn, automatically feeds back to our *self-esteem*. After all, what could be better than being noticed and confirmed in one's efforts? And then also by oneself!

So develop an awareness of the small and big things that do you good and that you want to treat yourself to in good time. This can be the conscious break in which it's just you and your delicious latte. Or a bouquet of flowers that you give yourself. Or maybe you'll treat yourself to a trip to the movies or that new watch you've been eyeing for a long time.

Body Language

Whether you realize it or not, your body speaks volumes. A person's body language usually gives a very clear indication of how they feel about themselves and their environment. We all unconsciously send out signals through our posture, gestures and facial expressions and also receive these from our environment.

When we become aware of the power our body language has on our sense of self and the shaping of our relationships, we can begin to use it purposefully.

What your body says about you

If you've ever prepared for a job interview, you know that it often involves practicing a certain demeanor. If we want to convince a person we don't know yet of our worth - as in a job interview - we naturally try to come across as determined and self-confident as possible. In addition to a well-groomed appearance and mastery of common courtesies, job coaches then advise, among other things:

- Make sure your handshake is appropriate: not too weak (which could be interpreted as insecurity) and not too strong (which could be interpreted as a gesture of dominance).
- maintain eye contact to signal self-confidence
- to pay attention to an upright and open posture: Do not cross arms (interpreted as closed-mindedness); do not

"slouch" on chair (could be interpreted as lack of respect and discipline)

As artificial as this may seem when preparing for an interview, you unconsciously apply this knowledge in your everyday life. And you do so constantly. At least when it comes to perceiving and classifying the signals of other people. You will be familiar with this: A person who shuffles past you with a lowered gaze and drooping shoulders has a completely different effect on you than a person who crosses your path walking upright with a firm step and smiling directly at you. The latter seems more self-confident and probably also more likeable to you.

So how do you become such a person who walks through life upright, confident and smiling? If you are not already , well, there are some aspects you can pay attention to in order to optimize your appearance and your external impact.

Powerful voice

The way someone speaks, quickly determines whether we listen to them spellbound or have to concentrate hard to understand them. Use this to your advantage. Practice developing a powerful voice. This means:

- speaking loudly and clearly
- finding a moderate pace of speech: not too fast and not too slow
- Using emphasis and deliberate pauses in speech when you want to emphasize what is being said

Train your voice. Practice at home in front of a mirror, record yourself and listen to it, or ask a friend/partner to listen to you and give you feedback on your vocal tone. If you want to develop your voice in a special way, you can also sing regularly, join a choir or book a few lessons with a so-called voice coach.

51

Well-groomed appearance

Always make sure you have a well-groomed appearance. Because as they say, first impressions count. Only a few seconds are enough for us to form a picture of a new person. The human brain works in such a way that it classifies new stimuli or new people into familiar structures as quickly as possible. This is what is known as "pigeonhole thinking". When we meet a new person, we put him or her into an existing pigeonhole, depending on our mindset and wealth of experience. This happens automatically and is normal.

Use this knowledge for yourself by consciously conveying a good first impression of yourself. And the first impression mainly refers to the outer appearance. Therefore, make sure that you appear well-groomed. This means being at least clean and neatly dressed. In addition, it can mean to emphasize your personal advantages, e.g. by emphasizing clothing, make-up for women, a fancy hairstyle, etc. You may find that your appearance affects not only those around you, but also yourself. If you pay attention to a well-groomed appearance, you will eventually perceive yourself as more attractive. This in turn affects your self-confidence.

Maintaining sports and friendships

You already know about another important element that changes your body image for the better: sports. By exercising regularly, you will improve your body image and thus your overall appearance. It is important that you find ways for yourself to incorporate a regular sports routine into your everyday life. Maintaining social contacts also has a significant impact on our self-esteem. It has been proven that people with a stable social network suffer less from stress and tend to even have a longer life expectancy. Friendships are empowering places where you can show up for who you are. Friends can strengthen and encourage us. Friends can help us get through tough times. Friends make us feel less alone. So, invest some of your time in maintaining existing friendships.

Of course, it's also a good idea to combine the two strengthening elements: Simply exercise regularly with your friends. Or join a sports club and make new friends this way.

Luck

Do you know the saying *"Everyone is the architect of his own happiness"*? Does that mean that everyone is responsible for their own happiness?

Don't we often think of luck as something that comes into our lives more or less by chance? We often say *"God speed!"* or wish a person *"Good luck!"*.

But the above-mentioned expression gives the impression that everyone can forge his own luck. Do we have any influence on the luck in our lives? A clear answer: Yes!

The perception of happiness or unhappiness is a topic that science has already devoted itself to intensively.

There is even a separate branch of research: happiness research. This defines happiness first of all as *"a positive sense of well-being, which can mean something different for everyone."*

Happiness is further characterized by the frequent occurrence of positive emotions with a simultaneous low occurrence of negative emotions. Furthermore, it has been determined that positive events and developments that we ultimately perceive as "happiness" lead to increased dopamine being released in our brain. This automatically makes us feel euphoric and increases our attention.

From a purely psychological point of view, this happens so that we learn what makes us feel good and repeat it if necessary. However, too many feelings of happiness are also not good for us.

Experiments with rats have shown that the permanent release of feelings of happiness puts the rats in a kind of state of intoxication. As nice as this sounds at first glance, it also meant that the animals, in their quest for happiness, failed to take care of their basic needs, such as eating, drinking, and sleeping. To prevent the same fate from befalling us humans, it is therefore quite healthy to enjoy happiness in small, regular doses.

But how do you achieve happiness? Is there some kind of recipe for forging your own happiness? Well, you can definitely consciously work on your focus and direct it towards attracting happiness into your life. Following is how you can best do this.

OPTIMISM AND POSITIVITY

The key to your happiness is to have an optimistic and positive outlook on life. That's because if you have a positive way of thinking, you automatically tend to focus on the good.

And those who focus on the good are more likely to see and also accept happy moments and encounters.

This is an essential prerequisite for experiencing happiness: You have to be at peace with yourself and the world to such an extent that you are also prepared to attract and accept happiness. You may be familiar with the saying, *"Someone is standing in the way of his own happiness."* That describes this phenomenon quite well. Because often happiness is already within reach, but someone simply cannot perceive it.

Remember the *mindset glasses* at the beginning of this guide? Everyone has their own individual perspective on the world, remember? This is decisive for which stimuli, events and opportunities we direct our focus on. Accordingly, an optimistic and positive attitude makes it easier to see, accept and experience the big and small happiness in your life. If the mindset glasses are colored rather negatively, many large and small moments of happiness will probably simply be overlooked.

Health benefits

Developing a positive mindset not only makes sense for your personal and professional success. With an optimistic attitude towards life, you invest in your health at the same time and can even influence your life expectation. It has been shown several times that optimism has a positive influence on blood pressure, blood sugar levels and the probability of cardiovascular disease, among other things.

The connection between body, mind and soul is not new. Psychosomatics, for example, is a medical discipline. It has made it its goal to understand and examine diseases in connection with psychological phenomena.

Today we know that stress, for example, has a significant influence on the development of and susceptibility to various diseases. This can be explained, among other things, by the fact that our body releases more cortisol when it is under stress. Cortisol is a stress hormone that has an inhibiting influence on the immune system. Therefore, if you manage to acquire a well-founded positive attitude towards life, you simultaneously make yourself less vulnerable to stress and other negative factors. In this way, you also keep your body's hormone levels in balance. And your body will thank you in the form of health and vitality.

Implement positive thoughts

Up to this point, you have already received many tips and suggestions with which you can increase your self-confidence and stimulate feelings of happiness. For example, you can consciously use sports, fun and nutrition to activate the release of feelings of happiness. The same applies to cultivating social relationships. You know that you can make yourself feel good by boosting your self-confidence. For example, by learning to focus on your strengths and positive aspects. In addition, being *self-aware* also causes an increase in your positive self-perception.

So, in summary, you could say that if you think positively, you act positively. Those who feel confident present themselves to the world in this way.

Developing a lasting positive outlook is a process. The more you engage in it, the more you will notice how your way of thinking also increasingly makes itself felt in your external world. An optimistically oriented mindset has the power to transform our entire lives. To realize why your thoughts are so powerful to the texture of your entire life, you need to understand the following: You radiate all your thoughts about yourself and the world into your environment. You are not aware of it. But it is happening. Permanently. And your environment reacts to it.

Law of attraction and positive energy

Have you ever heard of the law of attraction? "As within, so without." Is the essential idea behind it. It means that the thoughts and feelings we carry within us have significant influence on what shows up in our lives.

You can use this knowledge to consciously direct your focus on the positive. Because if you do that, you will not only perceive your life more positively. You are automatically more open to all the beautiful things, moments and can better perceive and take advantage of the opportunities and possibilities in your life. In addition, you also radiate your positivity to those around you and receive a corresponding response. Think about the effect posture and appearance have on unknown people. If you walk through the world with an upright gait, an open manner, and a direct smile on your face, you will receive completely different reactions from those around you than someone who is slumped over and evasive. All your inner thoughts, feelings, wishes, and fears are more or less radiated to your environment. And your environment reacts to these "vibrations" by reflecting them back to you in the same way.

Who carries good in itself, good happens to him. Who is negative, attracts negative. That is the formula. If you want to permanently align your mindset in the direction of happiness, success, and satisfaction, you should therefore acquire a basic positive perspective.

NEGATIVITY

To the same extent that a positive mindset has the effect of attracting happiness and success into our lives, a negative mindset has the opposite effect. Unfortunately, when we are exposed to negativity in our lives, it can quickly lead to a downward spiral of sorts. With a pessimistic worldview, we notice more of the negative aspects and bad developments. Both concerning ourselves and others. We then neither have a particularly positive image of ourselves, nor are we receptive to positive experiences. This in turn makes us feel confirmed in our negative view of the world. Getting out of this loop is not so easy and requires a conscious reorientation of our perspective.

How negativity pulls you down

For example, if a person has a rather negative mindset, the perception of their everyday life is shaped by it. This person looks through their negatively colored glasses and may not even notice events outside of this negative focus. I am sure you will know this. There are those days when you wake up already in a bad mood and during the course of the day your clouded view of the world is steadily confirmed: It's raining, you miss the bus, your colleague greeted you in an unfriendly way again and the canteen food was bad, too.

Sounds familiar? Well, do you think it's possible that many positive things also happened that day, but you didn't even notice them because of your attitude?

For example, you may not have noticed that you were smiled at at the bus stop or that your favorite seat in the cafeteria was kept free.

By putting on negative glasses in the morning, we sometimes make sure that the rest of the day turns out to be terrible. We might have perceived the day's events differently if we had slept in and been woken up by the sun. What do you think?

Sometimes it is not us who put on the negative glasses. People from our environment can also display a negative perspective and thus influence us. For example, by complaining or providing us with negative news. We may also have people in our environment who deliberately attack or criticize us. People who are characterized by a pessimistic view of the world also view their environment in this way.

This can then become apparent in their behavior towards us. So if you have negative people in your environment, take good care of yourself. After all, it is not so easy to display a positive perspective when you are confronted with the negativity of others.

Dealing with criticism

If you are confronted with criticism from outside in your life, the first step you should take is to become aware of it: Not all criticism is justified, and sometimes a critical word comes only from another person's critical perspective. Regularly realize that criticism of your person always reveals a statement about the critic's worldview.

Let's assume you have a very critical boss who is particularly ruthless with you. Then, as a first step, you should become aware that this boss probably also views himself and his world from a very critical perspective. This knowledge can help you maintain your fundamentally positive attitude. At the same time, make sure that critical words don't get the power to shake your belief in yourself. We tend to take criticism very personal and feel that our whole person is being questioned.

However, you can learn to reinterpret criticism. Because regardless of the perspective of the person criticizing, every criticism also always holds potential for learning about yourself. Therefore, try the following: Understand critical statements as a mirror of yourself and learn from them. According to the law of attraction, a part of you has arranged to have a certain criticism mirrored to you on the outside. For example, *"You work way too slowly. You need to improve your work process!"* Maybe a part of you thinks the same thing. Or you have unconsciously contributed to having this theme mirrored by your boss.

Therefore, use every criticism also to check for yourself whether there is some truth in it. And if so, what you can do to solve this issue. In this case, you could, for example, become aware that your work process could run more smoothly. You might then consider strategies for achieving greater efficiency.

So when you look at it this way, criticism is not a bad thing, but rather offers potential to improve and develop yourself.

HELPFUL TIPS FOR POSITIVE THOUGHTS

At this point, at the latest, you know all the good reasons for adopting a positive worldview. In order to develop this more and more and to direct your life in the direction of happiness, satisfaction and success in the long term, pay attention to the following aspects:

- Learn to be aware of your thoughts:

To permanently align your focus in a positive way, you must first become aware of your ongoing thought patterns. Try to get a sense of the way you view the world. If you become aware of negative thought patterns, you can then consciously undo them. Helpful methods for becoming aware of your thoughts include mindfulness exercises, meditation, or yoga.

- Get yourself into a positive mood:

Use the knowledge you have acquired so far. Work on your self-esteem, exercise regularly, eat consciously, maintain your social contacts, have fun.

- Shift your focus specifically to the positive:

Get into the habit of focusing on the positive aspects of your life. You can easily train this. For example, use positive affirmations regularly to do this. Keep a positive diary in which you record only positive experiences of the day every evening. Be aware of your strengths and successes and write them down.

- Distance yourself from the influence of negative people:

If possible distance yourself from negative people as good as you can. Either physically or at least mentally. Don't allow other people to question you or your positive outlook on life.

- Be a good friend to yourself:

Try to treat yourself like a good friend. Talk well to yourself instead of putting yourself down. Give yourself a present. Treat yourself. Be patient with yourself. Just be kind to yourself.

Self-discipline

THE SELF

We have used the term *self* several times in this guidebook. *Self-awareness*, for example, has been used to describe the ability to be *aware of one's self*. Remember? You intuitively knew what was meant by it when you read it, didn't you?

But what exactly does psychology mean when it talks about the "self"? How would you define your "self"? At this point, it's time to take a closer look at the concept of "self." According to the Online Encyclopedia of Psychology and Education:

"The "self" is a central concept for psychology when dealing with the human psyche, since the "self" comprises the totality of all conscious and unconscious aspects of the personality and generally strives for harmonization between them."

By the "self", then, we mean the summary of all our aspects and parts. Our "self" is what we conceive as our "I": What makes us tick, what we like, what our needs are, how we were shaped, and so on.

In case you just stumbled upon the idea that your "self" is supposed to be made up of different parts - yes, that's right.

Psychology assumes that every person - every "self" - is made up of different personality parts. You need not worry. This is not an indication of a mental abnormality. Rather, it is the result of a completely normal developmental process.

During our life and growing up, we are confronted with the most different reference persons and contexts. Depending on their importance for our life situation, they shape us to a greater or lesser extent. Our "self" - that is, what we finally understand as our "I" - develops through the exchange and feedback in all these interactions and situations that we experience and have experienced. The "self" reflects who we have learned to be. To put it more precisely:

A child is significantly shaped by his or her core family. This includes mother, father, possibly siblings, and grandparents. In addition, a child is integrated into a wide social network consisting of friends, educators, teachers, other parents, coaches and so on.

With each of these people, the child has a specific relationship. In the process of growing up, it learns through communication and feedback from its environment:

- who he is and how he is seen
- what the world is like
- how relationships work and are formed

Depending on how his caregivers understand themselves and the world, they convey a specific imprint to the child. For example, the child could grow up with a loving mother who is devoted to him. From its interaction with her, it will then tend to derive a positive self-image. But it could also be that the child regularly spends time with his demanding grandparents. These may be more likely to give him a sense of being flawed because they are difficult to please. The child now builds up an image of who he or she is over the course of his or her life from all these experiences and feedback about himself or herself. The "self" comes into being.

In this "self", all the different experiences with his environment are finally mapped. Different inner parts emerge. So, it can come to the following: There may be an inner part that is courageous and sets great goals for itself. At the same time, there may be a part that criticizes and badmouths all these goals.

Do you know something like this? The existence of different, contradictory inner parts is usually the cause of inner conflicts, learning and motivation blockades. The problem is that we are usually not aware of which parts are in us and what goals and motives they may be pursuing.

Normally, however, we don't notice much of this. After all, that is what makes up our Self - it brings all the different parts into harmony and thus defines our personality.

THE DISCIPLINE

The term "discipline" stems fromLatin ("disciplina") and translates as "teaching, discipline, (systemic) order". The Encyclopedia of Values defines discipline as:

"a) the observance of certain rules, prescribed rules of conduct, or the like; the conforming to the order of a group, a community.

b) the control of one's own will, feelings and inclinations in order to achieve something".

In the context of this guidebook, the second definition is especially important. Discipline, then, describes the ability to control one's will, feelings and inclinations to such an extent that one manages to achieve a certain goal. Discipline is therefore an essential quality for the realization of our plans. It means directing all one's energy towards having something in one's life and not allowing oneself to be distracted by either external or internal factors.

WHY DO WE NEED SELF-DISCIPLINE

Self-discipline - *the discipline of our self* - is an essential element in achieving our goals. Without the necessary degree of discipline, it is not possible to discard old patterns or learn something new. Therefore, on the way to your unlimited mindset, you need sufficient self-discipline.

People are creatures of habit. You surely know this sentence, don't you? From the field of educational research we know that things have to be repeated several times for a person to internalize them. It gets even more complicated when we want to "overwrite" an old pattern. It takes many, regular repetitions until we have acquired a new routine.

For example, you might set a goal to incorporate a sports routine into your daily routine. Let's say you want to jog three times a week for 30 minutes. Then it will take you a few weeks - maybe even months - to build the routine into your daily life to the point where you perceive and live it as a matter of course. How many of these regular repetitions you must have performed by then cannot be said in general terms. The ability to adopt a new routine or way of looking at things depends very much on the individual person.

Whether it is developing new routines or learning new skills (such as a foreign language), it cannot be done without self-discipline. We can understand self-discipline as a kind of "self-control competence", which is responsible for directing all the different inner parts towards achieving the set goal. In this context, the following phrase can also be understood: *"Overcoming your inner demons."*

The *inner demon* can be understood as a part of you that has no interest in great effort. It's at work when you look out the window in the morning, see that it's raining, and say to yourself *"Oh, jogging, I can do that tomorrow. Or the day after."*

You probably know this phenomenon, right? We all carry a more or less big *inner demon* in us. The crucial question is whether we give in to it or what we can do to counter it. And that's where self-discipline helps us.

WHAT DO WE CHANGE WITH SELF-DISCIPLINE

It has been scientifically proven that life-satisfied people are characterized by two qualities above all: Intelligence and discipline. Furthermore, strong self-discipline has positive effects on a person's health, wealth, and success. This makes sense. Because we need self-discipline to advance our development and break old patterns.

Having goals and developing visions is one thing. But if we don't take action, or if we don't succeed in keeping our *inner demon* in check, they will remain just that: goals and visions. Unrealized dreams and castles in the air. Probably accompanied by the bad taste of having failed.

In order to actively shape and reshape our lives, we must be able to discipline our "self". Intelligence is good. Talent is great. But both alone will not lead you to reach your goal. Unless there is enough perseverance behind it to persistently work toward a goal, it doesn't matter how talented you may be. What really matters is that you begin to act and actively move toward your goals. This requires, above all, the application of strength and energy to constantly "stay on the ball." Self-discipline is therefore one of the linchpins for creating your successful, happy, and fulfilling life.

IDENTIFY YOUR "WHY"

In order to muster the long-term energy, you need for a new endeavor, you need a plan. An essential part of this plan is good arguments. You can then counter your *inner demon* or other critical parts when your discipline is at a low. Because let's not fool ourselves. Discipline lows are part of it. If you know this, you can develop a strategy to deal with them in advance.

In addition to having a clear goal of what you want to achieve, it is extremely helpful to be aware of your personal "why". Every goal is based on at least one deep inner need or motive. Be aware of this. And keep it in mind regularly. Imagine in the most dazzling colors what your life will be like when you finally achieve your goal. How will you be? How will you feel? What will you look like? Who will be with you? Go ahead and really indulge in dreaming this vision of yourself. This will give your self-discipline a new boost to want to achieve this goal.

If your deepest inner "why" isn't even that present yet, you can use the following questions to help you determine it:

- Why is this particular skill or trait so important to me?
- Do I want to achieve the goal primarily for myself or for someone else?
- What do I expect to gain from achieving my goal?

- What changes will occur in my life as a result?
- To what extent will my life improve when I have achieved my intention?

FIVE IMPORTANT FACTORS

The following factors play a significant role in developing and maintaining self-discipline.

Distraction

The biggest enemy on the path to achieving our goals is distraction. There are many different ways you can distract yourself - consciously or unconsciously - from achieving your goals. On the one hand, there are the many, supposedly small time wasters in our everyday life, with which we can distract ourselves wonderfully: Cell phone, television, internet, Facebook, Instagram, YouTube. In our modern, technologically structured everyday life, it has become a challenge not to be constantly available or up to date.

Perhaps you know this: You have set yourself a daily goal, for example to write a five-page text. Before that, you want to take a quick look at Facebook to see what's new. And then your friend sends you a voice message to which you have to reply. You quickly read the news online again. And suddenly an hour has passed. And you haven't written a word. Annoying.

It's important to be aware of how many sources of distraction we automatically access in our daily lives. If you have set yourself a specific goal, it makes sense to cut yourself off from these sources of distraction for a fixed period of time. For example, by simply switching off your cell phone. Many people nowadays also allow themselves deliberate *"social media detox"* - phases in which they don't use their social media channels.

In addition to the aforementioned everyday time wasters, there are a variety of other distractions. Basically, there are about as many ways to distract yourself as there are goals to achieve. You may also be familiar with the phenomenon of "Oh, I need to clean my apartment before I can start working." And bang, half the workday is over. Or you still have to help your friend, wash the car, cut your hair and so on and so forth. Everything that comes to your mind when you are actually about to start in the direction of your goal is distracting behavior. Responsible for this is some inner part of you - in case of doubt your inner demon.

Habits

It has already been mentioned above: People are creatures of habit. That's how it is. For you this means: If you want to learn or develop something new, make a habit out of it. Practice and perform the new habit regularly. Whether it's learning an instrument or wanting to think more positively. Whether you want to develop a sports routine or boost your self-confidence. The important thing is that you make a habit of it.

It's best to create set periods of time for this, dedicated only to learning the new skill or routine. Schedule them into your daily routine. Put them in your calender, if necessary. For example, if you want to work on thinking more positively, schedule a fixed window of time each day to practice this (for example, using a positive diary or affirmations). If you want to exercise regularly, schedule time slots in your daily routine to do so. If necessary, create a weekly schedule in which you determine when you will exercise.

If you integrate new habits into your everyday life in this way and practice them regularly, they will become second nature to you over time. Your *inner demon* will then automatically not bother you that often because you have established the new skill or characteristic as a habitual routine for yourself.

Motivation

In order to work determined and persistently towards a goal, you also need a strong sense of motivation. It will come as no surprise to you at this point: without motivation, we lack the drive we need to learn something new.

Motivation can be expressed in many different ways. The basis of motivation is the pursuit of certain motives. In other words: we have certain motives that make us act purposefully. Usually, several motives underlie the pursuit of a certain goal.

We can distinguish between *extrinsic motivation factors* and *intrinsic motivation factors*. Extrinsic motivation refers to external factors. Intrinsic motivation factors are equivalent to your personal and innermost motives that underlie the pursuit of a goal. Let's assume that your goal is to be very successful professionally. Then you probably associate several motives with this:

Extrinsic motives could be that you hope to gain more social prestige through your success or that you will then be able to afford certain status objects (such as a big house or a fancy car).

Intrinsic motives could be that you want to contribute your expertise to a greater degree; or perhaps you have a need to prove something to yourself.

When we set a certain goal, we have a certain basic motivation anyway. However, this diminish or become less along the way to achieving our goal. There are some ways in which we can then motivate ourselves.

These will be described in the further course of this guide.

Since the topics "motivation" and "self-motivation" are extremely relevant for the development of a successful mindset, the following chapter is dedicated to a detailed presentation.

Preparation

Maintaining self-discipline also requires good preparation. This is characterized on one side by being aware of your goals and developing a realistic plan for how to achieve them. Furthermore, good preparation includes being a little ahead of yourself to be prepared for any eventuality.

Good planning includes knowing that there will be fluctuations within your pursuit of your own goal, discipline and motivation. So, consider your personal pitfalls and develop strategies to deal with them well. This may include, for example, becoming aware of your distractors and eliminating them. It may also mean creating a good and tidy work environment from the start or creating a set plan for practicing routines.

Willpower

Ultimately, of course, willpower determines the extent to which we can maintain our self-discipline. The stronger your need to achieve something, the more you are willing to put in the necessary effort. Willpower is closely related to motivation. However, the two differ as follows:

While motivation is crucial to our willingness to *want* to achieve and do something, willpower is the drive that ultimately makes us act and "get things done." How strong-willed we are is already inherent in our genes. However, willpower can also be trained wonderfully. You can do this by repeatedly setting yourself small or large challenges and mastering them. There are many ways in your everyday life to leave your comfort zone and to grow yourself.

For example, you can resolve to take a cold shower every morning. Or to pay a compliment to a stranger. Or try a new sport. Or to do something else that at the first moment needs a little overcoming. With each of these experiences, you learn that you can cope with unfamiliar situations. This strengthens your willpower.

STEPS TO MORE SELF-DISCIPLINE

To summarize, the following steps can be taken to increase your self-discipline:

Set clear goals

Be aware of your goals and formulate them clearly and realistically. In the case of large goals, break them down into small subgoals. Write these goals down and place them in a visible place: preferably at your workplace; you may also have a board on which you can record your goals.

It is important that you regularly confront yourself with your goals in everyday life in order to maintain your self-discipline. Also, feel free to practice visualizing your goal state on a regular basis: What will your life be like when you have achieved your goals? How will you feel?

By regularly putting yourself in this state, you will create a new drive for yourself. In this way, it will be easier for you to contradict your *inner demon* and continue working towards the realization of your goals.

Be aware of your motivational factors

It also has a similar effect if you make yourself aware of your motivational factors and regularly visualize them. Here again the questions to work out your personal "why":

- Why is this particular skill or characteristic so important to me?
- Do I want to achieve the goal primarily for myself or for someone else?
- What do I expect to gain from achieving my goal?
- What changes will occur in my life as a result?
- To what extent will my life improve when I have achieved my intention?

Write down these answers as well and visualize your future actual state on a regular basis. The resulting maintenance of your motivation will directly affect the maintenance of your self-discipline.

Eliminate distracting factors

Become aware of your personal distraction factors and turn them off. Create fixed spaces where you dedicate yourself to working on your goals.

Unless absolutely necessary, deactivate traditional sources of distraction such as cell phones, the Internet, and telephones during these times. It can also be a strategy, for example, to block yourself from certain Internet sites (such as Facebook).

In addition, become aware of possible sources of distraction and, if possible, do not give in to them either. Become aware of what comes to your mind when you are actually planning to work on the realization of your goal. Be aware of this and create an alternative space for it. Say, for example, "Yes, that's right, I really need to vacuum again. Right now, though, I'm going to work my scheduled three hours first. After that, I'll schedule a half hour to vacuum."

Work on your willpower

Create small challenges for yourself that you can grow from. Increase your belief in yourself this way. Navigate your focus toward success in this way already.

For example, create a list of things that you would like to do, but which initially involves some overcoming for you. You can then create small challenges for yourself, for example daily or weekly challenges. Examples could be:

This week I would like to ...

- smile at an unknown man.
- pay a compliment to an unknown woman.
- meditate every morning.
- go out the door dressed in a flashy way.
- go to that new dance class.
- refuse a request.

Find allies and role models

A real secret recipe for increasing your self-discipline is to have people in your life with the same or similar goals.

If you want to lose weight, for example, this is immensely easier once you have allies. You can then motivate yourself to exercise together, exchange ideas about nutrition and motivate each other during low points. Shared sorrow is halved, as the saying goes. Or shared joy is double joy. It can also be similarly motivating if you find a role model for yourself who has already successfully followed the path you are striving for.

For example, this could be someone who has achieved professional success in the way you would like. You can then engage with this person and follow their career path as best you can. Or you can even establish a personal contact in order to exchange ideas and be inspired by their personal experiences. Perhaps you can also receive concrete tips or expand your network in this way.

Reward yourself

With all the effort, discipline and constant self-motivation, don't forget one crucial thing: Be kind and patient with yourself. Value yourself and your effort. Reward yourself regularly for what you do. This includes giving yourself conscious breaks on a regular basis. But you should also treat yourself to concrete gifts. Buy yourself a bouquet of flowers if you feel like it or go out for dinner.

If you have reached one of your goals or subgoals, it may also be the new necklace or the new cell phone. Keep reminding yourself of all the things you are willing to do for yourself. What efforts you take upon yourself, to work towards a more fulfilling life.

You deserve to thank yourself for it. Not just because it keeps you motivated. But above all because you are worth it.

Motivation

Why does motivation play a big role in everyday life?

The previous chapter already pointed out the great importance of motivation. Since it not only has an influence on self-discipline, but is of equally great value in its significance for mindset work, this chapter is devoted to a detailed presentation of motivation. For this purpose, it first makes sense to refer to a precise definition of the term. The Online Lexicon for Psychology and Education defines motivation as follows:

"Motivation refers to processes in which certain motives are activated and converted into actions. This gives behavior a direction towards a goal, a level of intensity and a sequence of events. A person's motivation to pursue a particular goal depends on situational incentives, personal preferences, and their interaction."

Motivation, then, is the basis for impulses to act. It is the driving force for the goals we set for ourselves and the behavior we strive for. The intensity of motivation depends on personal and situational conditions. You already know the importance of intrinsic and extrinsic motivation factors from the previous chapter.

Now take a look at your normal everyday life. For example, let today pass before your inner eye. What role does motivation play in your everyday life? What tasks do you have to accomplish? How do you handle them? Do you enjoy them? Or do you also know moments when individual tasks stress you out or you need more time for them than for others?

The key to all this is motivation. Surely, it has become clear to you that successfully managing your everyday life is impossible without a minimum level of motivation. For example, you get up in the morning and go to work. For most of us, work plays a major role in our daily routine. You will probably also know that you are not equally motivated to work every day. Sometimes you can't wait to be at work, while on other days you would rather lie in bed a little longer. I assume that you also have a variety of different motives for going to work. You probably like to occupy yourself with your profession because it corresponds to your interests. That is a classic *intrinsic motive*. Then you may have great colleagues with whom you enjoy exchanging ideas.

But it could also be that you don't really identify yourself with your job, but you earn a lot of money or have access to a fancy company car. In this case, you would be primarily *extrinsically motivated*; you would work primarily to get something from the outside in return.

In addition, there can be several other large and small motives, such as the fact that your employer is within walking distance, that you have been employed there for a long time, that you are working towards an internal, higher position, and so on and so forth. The fact is, as soon as you lose your motivation, it will cost you considerably more energy to do your work every day. Because motivation is the driving force for performance.

When we are motivated to deal with something, it is easy for us and we can grow beyond ourselves. If we lack motivation - you will certainly know this - it can be torture to turn to a subject. So as a short formula you can remember: The more motivation, the more performance, the more success.

WHAT HAPPENS TO THE MIND AND BODY?

When we are motivated and our everything feels like a piece of cake for us, it has a significant impact on our overall condition. Motivation is what makes our life meaningful. When we lack motivation to accomplish our everyday tasks; when we have no goals in life to work towards - we become ill.

This can manifest on a mental-emotional level, for example in the form of depressive thoughts. But it can also become visible in our bodies, as we feel depressed, tired or exhausted, and coping with our daily lives demands enormous strength from us. When people are confronted with mental or physical blockages, it is usually a matter of taking a closer look at their own lives. It may then turn out that there is a lack of fundamental identification with one's own living conditions. Then it is often the task to carefully redesign one's own life and to steer it in a different direction. The following questions, among others, play a role in this process:

- What is good for me, what do I like to do?
- Am I happy in my job, my relationship, etc.?
- What do I want to occupy myself with, what interests me?
- How should my life be, what makes me happy?

It is then a matter of (re)discovering the inner motives and goals. By bringing these into consciousness, an orientation for the further shaping of life can emerge. New meaning can be created and experienced.

In order to keep your mind and body healthy, it is therefore important that you find sufficient motivation in your life. Should you ever notice that you are increasingly suffering from apathy or physical exhaustion symptoms, it is worth taking a look at your motivational factors. For this purpose, compare the way you live your life with the questions mentioned above. In this way, you can become aware of motivational blockages and take steps to increase or restore your motivation.

WHAT MOTIVATES US?

Motivation is the driving force for your performance and success - you already know that. You have also already learned that there are many factors that can have a motivating effect on us. Further above it has already been shown that all these different motives can basically be differentiated into:

intrinsic motivational factors

and

extrinsic motivational factors.

Intrinsic motivation factors are all those that come out of yourself. The prime example of intrinsic motivation has already been mentioned: Interest or passion for a certain topic. In addition, intrinsic motivation basically describes everything you want to do for yourself. The incentive for your actions lies within yourself. For example, you do sports because it's good for you.

Or you tidy up your apartment because it makes <u>you</u> feel better. Or you make your partner happy because it makes <u>you</u> happy.

Extrinsic motivational factors, on the other hand, relate to the outside world. The incentive for your actions therefore comes from the outside. This means everything that you do because of external factors. For example, a good salary or the recognition of colleagues can be extrinsic motives in your professional life. Or you do sports because <u>your partner</u> thinks you are too heavy and not because you want to do it yourself. Or you clean up your apartment because <u>your parents</u> come to visit. All of these are extrinsic motivational factors that drive us to take a certain action.

Intrinsic and extrinsic motivational factors both influence our capacity to want to do something.

However, they differ in their basic nature. And thus, also in how strong their effects are on our actual motivation and implementation of action.

WHAT HELPS WHEN THE SPORTS ARE MISSING?

Imagine the following example: You are doing a job that fulfills you absolutely. It corresponds to a high degree to your professional interests; you can develop and grow there and thus experience a sense of purpose in the performance of your work. At the same time, your salary is comparatively low and the social recognition for your profession is moderate.

Now you have an acquaintance who practices a profession that is associated with a certain status. When you meet new people together and he tells you about his job, he immediately attracts the glances and interest of everyone. Moreover, he earns a lot of money and can adorn himself with one or another status object. However, from conversations with him you know that he is not really enthusiastic about his work from a professional point of view. He does it because it allowed him to follow in his father's footsteps. Lately, he also often reports excruciating boredom and fatigue.

What do you think I'm trying to get at with this example? Right. To the fact that there are different underlying levels of motivation here. While you in our example are clearly intrinsically motivated and therefore find your work and your life fulfilling, your fictitious acquaintance may be suffering from an imbalance. Although he supposedly has everything you could wish for in terms of external motivational factors (= money, prestige, status objects), he seems to lack one essential aspect, namely: intrinsic motivation.

In fact, we know that intrinsic motivational factors can influence our sense of motivation to a considerably greater extent than extrinsic ones. Don't get me wrong: extrinsic motivational factors are good and important. But if, at the same time, there are no intrinsic motivators to achieve a certain goal, it is not possible to maintain motivation permanently. What good is it to have money, recognition and two Porsches in the garage if deep down you can't identify with what you are doing?!

Consciously setting yourself incentives to motivate yourself is basically always a goal-oriented way. And if you also look to extrinsic motives to achieve your goals, that's a good strategy. The need for recognition or the desire to be able to adorn yourself with a fancy car are legitimate motives that can also carry you in the direction of your goal for a while. However, to keep your incentive going in the long run, it means: Identify and strengthen your intrinsic motivational factors! Because these are the main drivers of your sense of motivation.

INCREASE INTRINSIC

MOTIVATIONIn order to maintain the perseverance you need to achieve your goals, it is important to know how to increase your intrinsic drive. In this context, it makes sense to become aware of your *intrinsic motives*. You can also make a note of them and place them in a clearly visible place. Once you have become aware of your personal motives for achieving your goals, you have access to the most powerful driving force.

According to motivation psychologists, three essential factors influence the fact that we feel intrinsically motivated. So, you can also consciously turn the following adjusting screws if you feel that you have a lack of intrinsic motivation:

- **Autonomy:**

The feeling of autonomy has a considerable influence on our motivation and thus also on our performance. Autonomy describes the feeling of personal responsibility and participation. It is the opposite of pure heteronomy. As soon as we have the feeling of having influence on our tasks and being able to shape them on our own responsibility, this also promotes our motivation. This is an important insight, especially in the context of employee motivation. Because according to this, it reduces performance if employees have the feeling that they have to act in a largely externally determined manner in their activities.

- **Mastery:**

People tend to strive for growth and further development. It is a good feeling to have improved or surpassed a previous performance. For this reason, games, championships and rankings have a strong appeal to us. Accordingly, it has a motivating effect when we have improved or learned something new. The prerequisite for this is that the progress is measurable and achievable. Goals that are set too high have a demotivating effect. However, if we can track our process using narrowly set subgoals, it increases our sense of motivation.

- **Purpose:**

Last but not least, it is of course of considerable importance for our sense of motivation that we see a purpose in our actions. If you can see meaning in your actions for yourself and/or the lives of others, that gives you a major motivational boost. It is therefore worthwhile to look inside yourself and become aware of the meaningfulness of the goal you are striving for.

STEPS TO MORE SELF-MOTIVATION

If you now want to motivate yourself in the best possible way, use the following aspects as a guide. Some of them are already familiar to you from the subchapter on increasing your self-discipline. This makes perfect sense, because both aspects are mutually dependent.

- **Develop visions:**

It has already been mentioned elsewhere. To develop and maintain your motivation, it is important that you have a vision. Take the time and space to visualize it as intensively as possible. Really dream yourself into your future life! How will you feel when you finally reach your goal? What will your life be like? Putting yourself in this mood will automatically increase your intrinsic motivation. True to the motto "That's what I want. That's where I want to go. That's who I want to be."

- **Identify motivational factors:**

In addition, determine your motivational factors. Write these down, perhaps initially in the form of a mind map. Write your goal in the middle and then collect all motivating aspects. Do not think about whether the motivation is intrinsic or extrinsic. Just collect them. Use the following questions as a guide:

- Why do I want to achieve the goal, what do I expect from it?
- What particularly appeals to me about the task / my goal?
- What sense/benefit does my goal have for me and/or others?

Then, in a further step, select extrinsic and intrinsic motives. In particular, write down your intrinsic motives and place them clearly visible.

- **Set realistic goals:**

Again, this closes the circle to what you have already experienced so far. Setting and visualizing goals is essential to motivate yourself. On one side, it is important to have goals in mind that you want to work towards. On the other side, the goals should be set in such a way that they are easily achievable. It therefore makes sense to divide a major goal into small-step milestones. This may also involve setting a precise timetable. If you set yourself a fixed time window with a deadline for a particular subtask, it can work wonders. We all know it: productivity increases under time pressure.

Basically, detailed planning supports the feeling that you can achieve your goals. In addition, you create the effect for yourself that you can make your progress visible. Both of these factors in turn have an effect on your motivation.

- **Rewarding yourself:**

It can't be said often enough. Give yourself regular, appropriate rewards for your commitment and perseverance. Make sure you take regular breaks. Go out to eat. Don't be afraid to give yourself a gift when you reach larger milestones. In this way, you'll keep creating small motivational incentives for yourself to keep going strong.

- **Think positively:**

And here, too, we've closed the circle. To maintain your motivation, it is essential to adopt a positive mindset. When you set goals, big or small, you will always come to points where things don't progress as you had hoped. You may also have to realign a goal because you hit limits of some kind. Or you simply have a hitch.

That's human and perfectly okay. The important thing is that you give up in such moments. Because it's precisely then that your positive mindset matters. Be gracious and patient with yourself. Don't beat yourself up even more. You won't achieve anything by doing so. At worst, it will extinguish your motivational fire.

HEALTH FOR BODY, MIND AND SOUL

It has already been pointed out, there is a connection between motivation, body, mind and soul. You can also influence this interaction in a very practical way: by eating consciously.

Healthy food for more motivation

To stay motivated and work persistently toward our goals, we need energy. On a mental level, we can ensure that we release and focus this energy. But we can also consciously control our energy balance with our diet. The way we eat has an enormous influence on how we feel in our bodies, how we think and how we perform.

In order to maintain our motivation and keep our entire system in a fit, efficient state, we need a balanced diet. So-called *brain food* ensures that we can concentrate better, perform better and strengthen our mental abilities. In a nutshell, it's about eating foods that provide you with energy for as long as possible. Unfortunately, reaching for a sweet or a cola only helps in the short term, as the energy level you have absorbed drops off again relatively quickly. Below are some foods that you should include in your diet to increase your motivation:

Motivational snacks

Nuts

Nuts are very effective providers of energy and protein. Both are important for the activity of your brain. Moreover, your body creates serotonin by consuming nuts. And we remember, serotonin is the happy hormone that automatically puts you in a better mood.

Berries

Berries are good sources of energy for your brain. Blueberries, in particular, boost your thinking ability.

Oatmeal/whole grain products

Oatmeal and whole grain products provide your body with magnesium, iron, B vitamins and long-chain carbohydrates, among others. This gives you plenty of long-lasting energy. For a good start to the day, combine oatmeal with nuts and berries, for example.

Avocados

Avocados are the new superfruits. And rightly so. Among other things, they contain lots of B vitamins and omega-3 fatty acids. In short, avocados lift your mood and give you lots of energy. You can add avocados to your diet in many ways: as a smoothie, on bread, as a dip, in a salad. Let your creativity run wild.

Fish

Fish contains omega-3 fatty acids. And they are not only great for improving your mood, but also increase your concentration. Tuna, salmon and herring, in particular, should be a regular part of your diet.

Also make sure you drink plenty of water. Drink at least two liters of water a day to keep your body hydrated and your brain performing at its best.

MOTIVATION AT WORK

You now know the essential aspects with which you can influence your motivation. Everything that has been presented up to this point can also be referred to when it comes to maintaining and increasing your own motivation at work.

How to become more successful

You already know the formula for more success: The more motivation, the more performance, the more success. So now the question is how you can shape your professional success in concrete terms. To do this, follow the steps outlined for achieving increased motivation. Develop visions of what you want to achieve professionally, identify your motivational factors and set realistic goals. Be sure to develop and maintain a positive outlook.

Don't be put off by critical voices. Encourage and reward yourself. Also pay attention to the extent to which the three essential motivational factors of autonomy, mastery and purpose are reflected in your life. If these have been given too little space so far, try to find ways to implement them. For example, talk to your boss and find out where you can be given more leeway. Challenge yourself, for example, by continuing your education and developing your professional skills.

Start your drive to learn

In order to take concrete action, make sure you set realistic goals. Create time schedules. Divide your goal or task into small milestones and set a specific time period for each subgoal. Think about how you will reward yourself when you reach the (stage) goals and then implement this in the same way. Then identify your sources of distraction and eliminate them. Allow yourself breaks. Plan for them as part of your schedule. Have access to brain food. Hang up your noted goals and motives in a clearly visible place at your workplace.

Motivate yourself and colleagues

It is also particularly effective to include your colleagues in your motivation strategies and to motivate each other. It has been shown that positive, collegial interaction is one of the main motivating factors for employees. Take advantage of this! Be appreciative and motivate each other. Make sure your colleagues feel comfortable and that they also enjoy coming to work. Offer your help to a colleague if you feel they need it. Give each other feedback on your performance. Don't be afraid to give praise and compliments to your colleagues. Also ask for feedback on your professionalism when you feel like it. It may also include making your work environment more appealing. Think about what your environment would need to look like to make you feel more motivated. And then implement this after consulting with your superiors and your colleagues. This could be plants, pictures or motivational sayings. Perhaps certain office furniture or colorful office materials are also conceivable. Just make your workday as a whole nicer, more beautiful and more lively. After all, if you feel good at work, you'll enjoy going there, be more motivated and, accordingly, perform better.

MOTIVATE FRIENDS, FAMILY AND CHILDREN

Basically, of course, it makes sense if not only you yourself, but also your environment is positively minded and motivated. Think back to the influence of different ways of thinking. If you want to work permanently towards a positive, motivated attitude towards life, it has a positive supporting effect if your environment is also optimistic and full of drive to do something. And, of course, your friends, family and children will also benefit.

All the steps you use to motivate yourself can of course also be taken to those around you. You would then kill two birds with one stone: ensure a positive attitude in your loved ones and create a more solid foundation for your own. If that's not a reason to be intrinsically motivated!

Basically, you can take a cue from everything we've said so far. For example, if you have someone in your environment who is pursuing a specific goal, support them in successfully tackling it.

It doesn't matter if your child has to study for a class test, your partner wants to develop professionally or your mother wants to lose weight:

- Offer your help, but don't impose.
- Provide incentives for setting proper goals.
- Assist in creating timelines.
- Assist in working out motivational factors and willpower.
- Encourage.
- Praise and reward the big and small successes along the way to goal achievement.
- Point out the importance of balanced nutrition.
- Recommend this guidebook.

Be supportive through it all, but most importantly, don't patronize!

True and persistent motivation - as you now know - must come from within and requires feelings of autonomy and self-control. Accordingly, the motivation of your environment can only be about offering help for self-help. After all, expectations or demands from outsiders can have an opposite effect and create additional blockages.

Basically, you can take care to shape your life and that of your environment as positively as possible. Make sure you treat each other with appreciation. Do something on a regular basis to benefit from positive experiences together. Cook a balanced diet.

Be patient. Motivate each other in your projects. Focus on the good aspects of your everyday life. If you live in a positive environment, it's easy to shift your mindset towards optimism, motivation and success.

Closing words

Now you know all the important aspects that make up your powerful mindset. Even more: You are already in the middle of your process. You are already on your way to your fulfilled life!

You have learned how your mindset is linked to your way of thinking and you know the essential factors with which you can influence your way of thinking. You know how to consciously align your focus to develop your mindset to infinity.

Furthermore, you now have the necessary tools to successfully set goals. This is the beginning of any successful mindset transformation. You have been given a variety of tips with which you could experience to become *more aware of yourself*. In this way, you are empowered to formulate and implement your goals even more successfully. You also know the power of positive thinking and the law of attraction. And you know how to steer yourself towards establishing happiness and optimism as fixed parameters in your life. In order to successfully anchor all of this in your life, you have also received sufficient guidance on how to develop and increase your self-discipline and motivation.

You know how important it is to be aware of your inner motives and to sharpen your willpower. And you have acquired a self-esteem and self-rewarding approach to yourself. Finally, in order to maintain your performance, concentration and physical health during all of this, you have the necessary know-how regarding nutrition, sports and holistic fitness.

Congratulations, you are ready! From now on it is only a matter of time until your wishes, dreams and visions will manifest in your life!

The Infinite Mindset

Learn why positive thinking, self-confidence, self-discipline and motivation, enriches your mindset and helps you evolve towards infinity.

For questions and suggestions:

berisha-sales@outlook.de

Edition 2020